~A BINGO BOOK~

Educational Books 'n' Bingo
EBB5302

Oregon Bingo Book

COMPLETE BINGO GAME IN A BOOK

STATE OF OREGON

THE UNION

1859

Written By Rebecca Stark

ISBN 978-0-87386-530-2

Educational Books 'n' Bingo

Printed in the U.S.A.

DIRECTIONS

INCLUDED:

List of Terms

Templates for Additional Terms and Clues

2 Clues per Term

30 Unique Bingo Cards

Markers

1. **Either cut apart the book or make copies of ALL the sheets. You might want to make an extra copy of the clue sheets to use for introduction and review. Keep the sheets in an envelope for easy reuse.**

2. Cut apart the call cards with terms and clues.

3. Pass out one bingo card per student. There are enough for a class of 30.

4. Pass out markers. You may cut apart the markers included in this book or use any other small items of your choice.

5. Decide whether or not you will require the entire card to be filled. Requiring the entire card to be filled provides a better review. However, if you have a short time to fill, you may prefer to have them do the just the border or some other format. Tell the class before you begin what is required.

6. There are 50 terms. Read the list before you begin. If there are any terms that have not been covered in class, you may want to read to the students the term and clues before you begin.

7. There is a blank space in the middle of each card. You can instruct the students to use it as a free space or you can write in answers to cover terms not included. Of course, in this case you would create your own clues. (Templates provided.)

8. Shuffle the cards and place them in a pile. Two or three clues are provided for each term. If you plan to play the game with the same group more than once, you might want to choose a different clue for each game. If not, you may choose to use more than one clue.

9. Be sure to keep the cards you have used for the present game in a separate pile. When a student calls, "Bingo," he or she will have to verify that the correct answers are on his or her card AND that the markers were placed in response to the proper questions. Pull out the cards that are on the student's card keeping them in the order they were used in the game. Read each clue as it was given and ask the student to identify the correct answer from his or her card.

10. If the student has the correct answers on the card AND has shown that they were marked in response to the *correct questions,* then that student is the winner and the game is over. If the student does not have the correct answers on the card OR he or she marked the answers in response to *the wrong questions,* then the game continues until there is a proper winner.

11. If you want to play again, reshuffle the cards and begin again.

Have fun!

TERMS INCLUDED

Agricultural

Basin and Range

Beaver

Border (-ed)

Tabitha Moffatt Brown

Cascade

Chief Joseph

Climate

Coast Range

Columbia Plateau

Columbia River

County (-ies)

Crater Lake

Douglas Fir

Dungeness Crab(s)

Eugene

Executive Branch

Fish (-ing)

Flag

Fort Astoria

Fur

Hazelnut

High Desert

Hudson's Bay Company

Industry (-ies)

Jory

Judicial Branch

Klamath Mountains

Legislative Branch

Lewis and Clark

Dr. John McLoughlin

Metasequoia

Mining (-ed)

Motto

Mt. Hood

Multnomah Falls

"Oregon, My Oregon"

Oregon Swallowtail

Oregon Territory

Oregon Trail

Pacific Golden Chanterelle

Pear(s)

Portland

River(s)

Salem

Seal

Thunder-egg(s)

Tribe (-s; -al)

Union

Willamette Valley

Additional Terms

Choose as many additional terms as you would like and write them in the squares. Repeat each as desired.
Cut out the squares and randomly distribute them to the class.
Instruct the students to place their square on the center space of their card.

Oregon Bingo

Clues for Additional Terms

Write three clues for each of your additional terms.

_____ 1. 2. 3.	_____ 1. 2. 3.
_____ 1. 2. 3.	_____ 1. 2. 3.
_____ 1. 2. 3.	_____ 1. 2. 3.

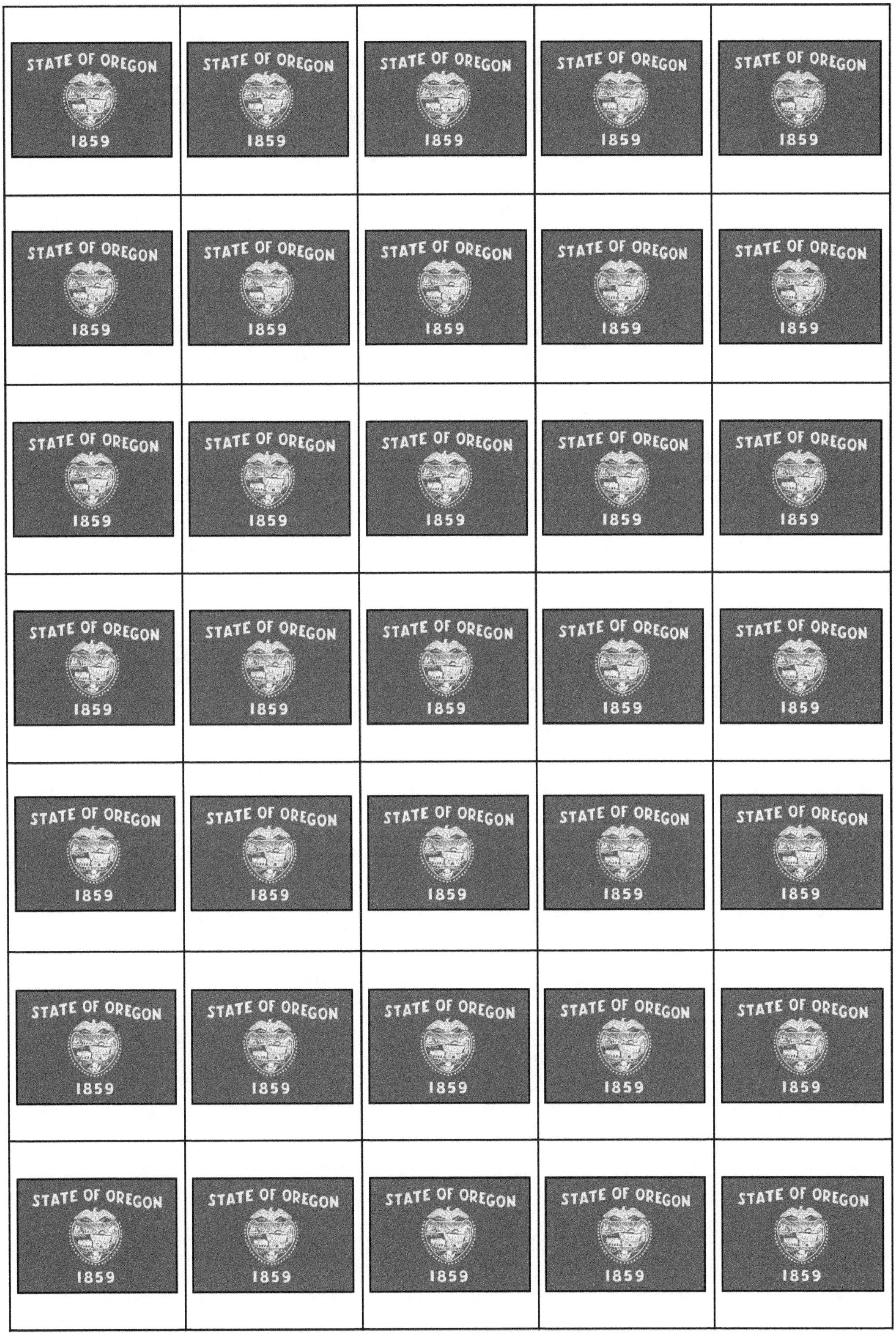

Agricultural
1. Important ___ products are greenhouse and nursery products, cattle and calves, dairy products, hay, and ryegrass.
2. Greenhouse and nursery products are the most important ___ products in terms of revenue, or income.

Basin and Range
1. The ___ Region covers southeastern Oregon. It gets only about ten inches of rain a year.
2. The ___ Region is characterized by high basins and a few steep mountains. Much of this region is semi-desert.

Beaver
1. The ___ is the state animal. In the 1800s, demand for its fur led to its virtual elimination in much of its original habitat.
2. Oregon is nicknamed the ___ State. The ___ is depicted on the reverse of the state flag.

Border (-ed)
1. Washington, California, Nevada, and Idaho ___ Oregon.
2. Oregon is ___ on the west by the Pacific Ocean. The Snake River forms the eastern ___ between Oregon and Idaho.

Tabitha Moffatt Brown
1. ___ is known as the "Mother of Oregon."
2. This pioneer woman financed her own wagon for the trip from Missouri to Oregon and established a boarding school for orphans.

Cascade
1. The ___ Mountains are east of the Willamette Lowlands. High peaks in this region include Mount Hood, Mt. Jefferson, Three Sisters, and Mount McLoughlin.
2. Crater Lake, the deepest lake in America, is in the ___ Mountains.

Chief Joseph
1. ___ was a leader of the Nez Percé. He became the symbol of Nez Percé heroism and resistance.
2. When ___ surrendered to General Miles, he delivered an eloquent speech. It ended with "I will fight no more forever."

Climate
1. The Cascade Mountains divide the state, producing two different ___ areas.
2. West of the Cascades, a mild, moist marine ___ prevails. East of the Cascades a drier, semi-arid ___ prevails.

Coast Range
1. The low mountain ranges of the ___ run from north to south along the Pacific Ocean.
2. In this region, cliffs rise almost 1,000 feet high over the Pacific Ocean. This region includes all but the southernmost part of the coast.

Oregon Bingo

Columbia Plateau
1. The ___ covers most of eastern Oregon and extends into Idaho and Washington.
2. The ___ is also known as the Columbia Basalt Plain. The Blue Mountains and the Wallowa Mountains rise in the northeast.

Columbia River 1. The ___ flows along most of the boundary between Oregon and Washington. 2. The ___ is the fourth-largest river in the United States and the largest of the Pacific Northwest.	**County (-ies)** 1. There are 36 ___ in Oregon. 2. Twenty-four of Oregon's 36 ___ are governed by a 3- to 5-member board of commissioners. The 12 less populated ones are governed by a judge and 2 commissioners.
Crater Lake 1. ___ is the deepest lake in America. It is depicted on the state quarter. 2. This lake in the Cascade Mountains is 1,932 feet deep.	**Douglas Fir** 1. The ___ is the state tree. 2. Oregon is the nation's leading producer of timber and plywood. The most important trees are the ___ and the ponderosa pine.
Dungeness Crab(s) 1. The ___ is the state crustacean. ___ live in coastal waters and thrive in estuaries. 2. About 10 million pounds of this crustacean are harvested each year.	**Eugene** 1. ___ is the second largest city in Oregon. It is located at the southern end of the Willamette Valley. 2. The University of Oregon is located in ___.
Executive Branch 1. The ___ comprises the governor, the secretary of state, the treasurer, the attorney general, and the commissioner of labor and industries. 2. The governor is head of the ___. The present-day ___ is [fill in].	**Fish (-ing)** 1. Commercial ___ is an important industry. Important catches include salmon, dungeness crab, pink shrimp, and albacore tuna. 2. The Chinook Salmon is the state ___. It is the largest of the Pacific salmons and the most highly prized.
Flag 1. The state ___ has a blue field with gold lettering and symbols. The front features the state seal surrounded by 33 stars. Above the shield are the words "STATE OF OREGON," and below it is the year 1859. 2. The reverse side of the state ___ depicts a beaver.	**Fort Astoria** 1. John Jacob Astor financed the establishment of ___ at the mouth of the Columbia River as a western outpost to his Pacific Fur Company. 2. ___ was the first permanent European settlement in Oregon.

Fur
1. ___ trappers blazed what would later be known as the Oregon Trail.
2. The demand for hats made of beaver ___ in the east was a factor in the early exploration of Oregon.

Hazelnut
1. The ___ is the state nut.
2. Oregon grows 99 percent of the nation's commercial crop of this nut.

High Desert
1. The ___ is east of the Cascade Range and south of the Blue Mountains in the central and eastern parts of the state.
2. The area known as the ___ is also called the Oregon Outback. In spite of its name, it is only arid compared to the western part of the state.

Hudson's Bay Company
1. The ___ began as a fur trading business. It is the oldest corporation in North America.
2. The ___ was founded in 1670 by English royal charter. It controlled the fur trade in the British colonies in America for several centuries.

Industry (-ies)
1. The manufacture of high-tech components is an important ___. Products include electronic equipment, printer components, microprocessors, and communication microchips.
2. The wood processing ___ is important. Manufactured products include plywood, veneer, and particleboard.

Jory
1. ___ is the state soil. It is ideal for various crops, including wine grapes, wheat, Christmas trees, berries, hazelnuts, and grass seed.
2. ___ supports forest vegetation, such as Douglas fir and Oregon white oak.

Judicial Branch
1. The ___ interprets what our laws mean and makes decisions about the laws and those who break them.
2. The Supreme Court is the highest court in the ___ of the state government. It reviews the decisions of the Court of Appeals in selected cases.

Klamath Mountains
1. The ___ are along the coast in the southwest corner of the state. They are covered by dense forests.
2. This rugged series of mountain ranges in southwestern Oregon is lightly populated. The ___ are sometimes called the Siskiyou Mountains.

Legislative Branch
1. The Assembly is the ___ of government. It comprises the Senate and the House of Representatives.
2. The ___ makes the laws.

Lewis and Clark
1. The ___ Expedition is also known as the Corps of Discovery. It was commissioned by President Jefferson to find a water route across North America and explore the uncharted West.
2. Fort Clatsop was the winter encampment for the ___ Expedition from December 1805 to March 1806.

Dr. John McLoughlin 1. ___ is known as the "Father of Oregon." 2. ___ came to the Pacific Northwest in 1824 as a representative of the Hudson's Bay Company. His mission was to monopolize the fur trade, keep peace with Indian tribes, and discourage agricultural settlement.	**Metasequoia** 1. The ___, or dawn redwood, is the state fossil. Although the least tall of the redwoods, it grows to over 200 feet. 2. ___ trees had been extinct in Oregon for years when living specimens were found in a remote area of China. Seeds were brought here and these trees are again in the state.
Mining (-ed) 1. About 75% of Oregon's ___ income is generated by sand and gravel for roadbeds and stone. 2. Other ___ products include pumice stone, clays, diatomite, gold, and semiprecious gems.	**Motto** 1. The state ___ is *"Alis Volat Propriis."* 2. In English the state ___ is "She flies with her own wings."
Mt. Hood 1. At 11,239 feet above sea level, ___ is the highest point in Oregon. It is in the Cascades. 2. The highest point in Oregon is ___. The lowest is sea level, where Oregon meets the Pacific Ocean.	**Multnomah Falls** 1. ___ is a waterfall on the Oregon side of the Columbia River Gorge. 2. ___ is the tallest waterfall in the state. It drops in two steps.
"Oregon, My Oregon" 1. ___ is the state song. 2. "Land of the Empire Builders" is the first line of ___.	**Oregon Swallowtail** 1. The ___ is the state insect. 2. This beautiful butterfly inhabits the lower sagebrush canyons of the Columbia River and its tributaries.
Oregon Territory 1. The ___ was officially organized in 1848. It comprised the current states of Oregon, Washington, and Idaho as well as parts of Wyoming and Montana. 2. The capital of the ___ was Oregon City, then Salem, then briefly Corvallis, and then Salem. Oregon Bingo	**Oregon Trail** 1. The ___ was an east-west wagon route and emigrant trail. It connected the Missouri River to valleys in Oregon and locations along the way. 2. This 2,000-mile wagon route brought many settlers to Oregon Country in 1842–1843. © Barbara M. Peller

Pacific Golden Chanterelle 1. The ___ is the state mushroom. 2. This wild, edible fungus is unique to the Pacific Northwest. The ___ represents a large portion of the commercial mushroom business.	**Pear(s)** 1. The ___ is the state fruit and the top-selling fruit crop in the state. 2. Oregon produces a variety of ___, including Comice, Anjou, Bosc, and Bartlett. They grow well in the Rogue River Valley and along the Columbia River near Mt. Hood.
Portland 1. ___ is the largest city in Oregon. The Willamette River runs through the center of this large city. 2. ___ is nicknamed "Rose City." The International Rose Test Garden is in this city.	**River(s)** 1. The Columbia, Deschutes, Willamette, John Day, and Snake are ___ in Oregon. 2. The Willamette ___ has 13 major tributaries and drains about 12,000 square miles. By volume, it is Oregon's largest ___.
Salem 1. ___ is the capital of Oregon. The Willamette River runs through the city. 2. ___ is the third largest city in the state after Portland and Eugene.	**Seal** 1. The Great ___ shows symbols of the state's history and resources, including mountains, forests, an elk, a covered wagon, the ocean, wheat, a plow, and a pickax. 2. The departing British man-of-war and the arriving American merchant ship on the Great ___ signify the departure of British influence and the rise of American power.
Thunder-egg(s) 1. The ___ is the state rock; however, it is not actually a rock. It is a structure called a geode. 2. These stones are made into beautiful jewelry, pendants, and other artifacts. They are found in central Oregon.	**Tribe (-s; -al)** 1. There are 9 federally recognized Native American ___ in Oregon.* 2. ___ members are citizens of their ___, of Oregon, and of the United States. *Burns Paiute Tribe; Confederated Tribes of Coos, Lower Umpqua, and Suislaw Indians; Confederated Tribes of Grande Ronde; Confederated Tribes of Siletz; Confederated Tribes of the Umatilla; Confederated Tribes of Warm Springs; Coquille Indian Tribe; Cow Creek Band of Umpqua Indians; and Klamath Tribe
Union 1. On February 14, 1859, President James Buchanan signed a bill that admitted Oregon into the ___. 2. The southwestern portion of Oregon Territory was admitted to the ___ as the thirty-third state. Oregon Bingo	**Willamette Valley** 1. Portland is at the northern end of the ___, Oregon's most populated region. 2. ___ is a narrow strip of land to the east of the Coast Range along the Willamette River, which flows north into the Columbia River. The soil in this region is rich and the climate is mild. © **Barbara M. Peller**

Oregon Bingo

Oregon Territory	Agricultural	Beaver	Flag	Tabitha Moffatt Brown
Executive Branch	Basin and Range	Tribe (-s; -al)	Lewis and Clark	Pear(s)
Thunder-egg(s)	Legislative Branch		Mt. Hood	Union
Multnomah Falls	Pacific Golden Chanterelle	Seal	Klamath Mountains	Metasequoia
Motto	Hazelnut	Douglas Fir	River(s)	Industry (-ies)

Oregon Bingo: Card No. 1

Oregon
Bingo

Oregon Bingo

Multnomah Falls	Thunder-egg(s)	Hudson's Bay Company	Oregon Trail	Judicial Branch
Metasequoia	Dungeness Crab(s)	Climate	Pacific Golden Chanterelle	Mining (-ed)
Columbia Plateau	Hazelnut		High Desert	Seal
"Oregon, My Oregon"	Oregon Swallowtail	Legislative Branch	Willamette Valley	Tabitha Moffatt Brown
Pear(s)	Tribe (-s; -al)	Douglas Fir	Executive Branch	River(s)

Oregon Bingo

Hazelnut	Seal	Dungeness Crab(s)	Klamath Mountains	Thunder-egg(s)
Metasequoia	Basin and Range	Coast Range	Agricultural	Fur
Pacific Golden Chanterelle	Tribe (-s; -al)		Mining (-ed)	Border (-ed)
Legislative Branch	Columbia Plateau	Motto	"Oregon, My Oregon"	Hudson's Bay Company
River(s)	Columbia River	Douglas Fir	Willamette Valley	Judicial Branch

Oregon Bingo

Legislative Branch	Mining (-ed)	Beaver	Columbia River	Judicial Branch
Dr. John McLoughlin	Chief Joseph	Agricultural	Oregon Trail	Thunder-egg(s)
Mt. Hood	"Oregon, My Oregon"		Industry (-ies)	Flag
Seal	Basin and Range	Tribe (-s; -al)	Douglas Fir	Climate
County (-ies)	Pear(s)	Cascade	River(s)	Union

Oregon Bingo: Card No. 4

Oregon Bingo

Pear(s)	Tabitha Moffatt Brown	Pacific Golden Chanterelle	Climate	Columbia River
Dr. John McLoughlin	Seal	Coast Range	High Desert	Basin and Range
Beaver	Union		Lewis and Clark	Fort Astoria
Industry (-ies)	Judicial Branch	Oregon Territory	Willamette Valley	Crater Lake
Dungeness Crab(s)	Douglas Fir	Thunder-egg(s)	Legislative Branch	Mt. Hood

Oregon Bingo: Card No. 5

Oregon Bingo

Border (-ed)	Mining (-ed)	Hudson's Bay Company	Judicial Branch	Union
Klamath Mountains	Pacific Golden Chanterelle	Crater Lake	Agricultural	Thunder-egg(s)
Oregon Trail	County (-ies)		Chief Joseph	High Desert
Douglas Fir	Motto	Willamette Valley	Cascade	Beaver
Metasequoia	Climate	Oregon Territory	Mt. Hood	Eugene

Oregon Bingo

Oregon Territory	Mining (-ed)	Fort Astoria	Seal	Dungeness Crab(s)
Metasequoia	Judicial Branch	Hazelnut	Basin and Range	Dr. John McLoughlin
Union	Flag		High Desert	Chief Joseph
Legislative Branch	"Oregon, My Oregon"	Coast Range	Multnomah Falls	Columbia Plateau
Douglas Fir	Columbia River	Willamette Valley	Cascade	Border (-ed)

Oregon Bingo: Card No. 7

Oregon Bingo

Mt. Hood	Mining (-ed)	Fish (-ing)	Klamath Mountains	Chief Joseph
Dr. John McLoughlin	Beaver	Oregon Trail	Union	Climate
Eugene	Columbia River		Judicial Branch	Tabitha Moffatt Brown
River(s)	Legislative Branch	Multnomah Falls	County (-ies)	"Oregon, My Oregon"
Tribe (-s; -al)	Douglas Fir	Cascade	Pacific Golden Chanterelle	Metasequoia

Oregon Bingo: Card No. 8

© Barbara M. Peller

Oregon Bingo

High Desert	Dungeness Crab(s)	Hazelnut	Eugene	Columbia River
County (-ies)	Judicial Branch	Mt. Hood	Pacific Golden Chanterelle	Mining (-ed)
Fur	Oregon Territory		Basin and Range	Fish (-ing)
Crater Lake	Tabitha Moffatt Brown	Motto	Lewis and Clark	Fort Astoria
"Oregon, My Oregon"	Willamette Valley	Coast Range	Multnomah Falls	Industry (-ies)

Oregon Bingo: Card No. 9

© Barbara M. Peller

Oregon Bingo

Multnomah Falls	Klamath Mountains	Chief Joseph	Oregon Trail	Eugene
Union	Climate	Agricultural	Basin and Range	Judicial Branch
Columbia River	Mining (-ed)		Flag	Columbia Plateau
Motto	Industry (-ies)	Crater Lake	Willamette Valley	Fur
Coast Range	Metasequoia	Hudson's Bay Company	Pear(s)	Mt. Hood

Oregon Bingo

Border (-ed)	Mining (-ed)	Pacific Golden Chanterelle	Crater Lake	Metasequoia
Fish (-ing)	Fur	Lewis and Clark	High Desert	Agricultural
Dr. John McLoughlin	Judicial Branch		Hudson's Bay Company	Hazelnut
Coast Range	Thunder-egg(s)	Willamette Valley	Columbia River	Multnomah Falls
County (-ies)	Douglas Fir	Oregon Territory	Cascade	Dungeness Crab(s)

Oregon Bingo: Card No. 11

Oregon Bingo

Dungeness Crab(s)	Tabitha Moffatt Brown	Fur	Klamath Mountains	High Desert
Hazelnut	Metasequoia	Beaver	Cascade	Basin and Range
Oregon Territory	Fort Astoria		Union	Oregon Trail
Douglas Fir	"Oregon, My Oregon"	Judicial Branch	Multnomah Falls	Dr. John McLoughlin
Mining (-ed)	Fish (-ing)	Columbia River	County (-ies)	Climate

Oregon Bingo

Crater Lake	Tabitha Moffatt Brown	Border (-ed)	Fur	Union
Beaver	Fish (-ing)	Judicial Branch	High Desert	Columbia Plateau
Klamath Mountains	Climate		Hazelnut	Fort Astoria
Mt. Hood	Willamette Valley	Chief Joseph	Columbia River	Multnomah Falls
Douglas Fir	Industry (-ies)	Cascade	Oregon Territory	Lewis and Clark

Oregon Bingo: Card No. 13

Oregon Bingo

Executive Branch	Judicial Branch	Pacific Golden Chanterelle	High Desert	County (-ies)
Climate	Oregon Territory	Fur	Basin and Range	Mining (-ed)
Crater Lake	Flag		Hudson's Bay Company	Coast Range
Industry (-ies)	Willamette Valley	Columbia River	Chief Joseph	Border (-ed)
Douglas Fir	Oregon Trail	Columbia Plateau	Metasequoia	Mt. Hood

Oregon Bingo

Lewis and Clark	High Desert	Pacific Golden Chanterelle	Dungeness Crab(s)	Klamath Mountains
Border (-ed)	Hudson's Bay Company	Agricultural	Beaver	County (-ies)
Union	Oregon Territory		Thunder-egg(s)	Mining (-ed)
Douglas Fir	Fur	Fish (-ing)	Willamette Valley	Crater Lake
Metasequoia	"Oregon, My Oregon"	Cascade	Eugene	Hazelnut

Oregon
Bingo

Oregon Bingo

Chief Joseph	Fur	Fish (-ing)	Eugene	Oregon Swallowtail
Oregon Trail	Columbia Plateau	Fort Astoria	Dr. John McLoughlin	Flag
Crater Lake	Tabitha Moffatt Brown		Union	Hazelnut
Legislative Branch	Climate	Douglas Fir	Lewis and Clark	Multnomah Falls
County (-ies)	Salem	Cascade	"Oregon, My Oregon"	Mining (-ed)

Oregon Bingo: Card No. 16

Oregon Bingo

Coast Range	Portland	Jory	Fur	Executive Branch
Lewis and Clark	County (-ies)	Willamette Valley	Flag	Fort Astoria
High Desert	Mt. Hood		Salem	Fish (-ing)
Industry (-ies)	Metasequoia	Multnomah Falls	Pacific Golden Chanterelle	Columbia Plateau
Motto	Crater Lake	Dungeness Crab(s)	Klamath Mountains	Tabitha Moffatt Brown

Oregon Bingo

Eugene	Columbia River	Climate	Crater Lake	Oregon Trail
Mining (-ed)	Coast Range	Motto	Union	County (-ies)
High Desert	Columbia Plateau		Jory	Beaver
Tabitha Moffatt Brown	Agricultural	Willamette Valley	Multnomah Falls	Hudson's Bay Company
Salem	Fur	Pacific Golden Chanterelle	Portland	Border (-ed)

Oregon Bingo

Union	Border (-ed)	Fur	Fish (-ing)	Multnomah Falls
Lewis and Clark	Klamath Mountains	Mining (-ed)	Dungeness Crab(s)	Flag
Portland	Columbia River		Basin and Range	Thunder-egg(s)
Hudson's Bay Company	Salem	Motto	"Oregon, My Oregon"	Jory
Beaver	Oregon Swallowtail	Metasequoia	Mt. Hood	Cascade

Oregon Bingo: Card No. 19

Oregon Bingo

Executive Branch	Portland	Klamath Mountains	Fur	Cascade
Climate	Hazelnut	Dr. John McLoughlin	Motto	Oregon Trail
Tabitha Moffatt Brown	Fort Astoria		Legislative Branch	Agricultural
Pear(s)	Tribe (-s; -al)	River(s)	"Oregon, My Oregon"	Salem
Seal	Mt. Hood	Oregon Swallowtail	Multnomah Falls	Jory

Oregon Bingo

Lewis and Clark	Border (-ed)	Dr. John McLoughlin	Fur	Pear(s)
Tabitha Moffatt Brown	Jory	Chief Joseph	Fish (-ing)	Oregon Territory
Columbia Plateau	Metasequoia		Portland	Pacific Golden Chanterelle
Motto	Dungeness Crab(s)	Salem	Industry (-ies)	Mt. Hood
Legislative Branch	Oregon Swallowtail	Cascade	Coast Range	"Oregon, My Oregon"

Oregon Bingo: Card No. 21

Oregon Bingo

Eugene	Hudson's Bay Company	Jory	Beaver	Crater Lake
Oregon Trail	Klamath Mountains	Thunder-egg(s)	Fish (-ing)	Basin and Range
Climate	Flag		Oregon Territory	Fort Astoria
Salem	Industry (-ies)	"Oregon, My Oregon"	Agricultural	Dr. John McLoughlin
Oregon Swallowtail	Coast Range	Portland	Columbia Plateau	Legislative Branch

Oregon Bingo

Chief Joseph	Portland	Dungeness Crab(s)	Beaver	Cascade
Border (-ed)	Executive Branch	Metasequoia	Lewis and Clark	Agricultural
Hudson's Bay Company	Crater Lake		River(s)	Oregon Territory
Columbia Plateau	Oregon Swallowtail	Salem	Coast Range	"Oregon, My Oregon"
Pear(s)	Tribe (-s; -al)	Mt. Hood	Motto	Jory

Oregon Bingo: Card No. 23

Oregon Bingo

Chief Joseph	Mt. Hood	Executive Branch	Portland	Fish (-ing)
Jory	Cascade	Dr. John McLoughlin	Oregon Trail	Oregon Territory
Fort Astoria	Eugene		Crater Lake	Columbia Plateau
Pear(s)	River(s)	Salem	Coast Range	Tabitha Moffatt Brown
Seal	Legislative Branch	Oregon Swallowtail	Klamath Mountains	Tribe (-s; -al)

Oregon Bingo

Legislative Branch	Dr. John McLoughlin	Portland	Pacific Golden Chanterelle	Jory
Agricultural	Tabitha Moffatt Brown	Lewis and Clark	Chief Joseph	Basin and Range
Industry (-ies)	Fish (-ing)		River(s)	Salem
Thunder-egg(s)	Pear(s)	Tribe (-s; -al)	Oregon Swallowtail	Flag
Cascade	Executive Branch	Climate	County (-ies)	Seal

Oregon Bingo: Card No. 25

Oregon Bingo

Jory	Portland	Hudson's Bay Company	Oregon Trail	Eugene
Motto	Klamath Mountains	Fish (-ing)	Executive Branch	Chief Joseph
Industry (-ies)	River(s)		Flag	Legislative Branch
Coast Range	Beaver	Pear(s)	Oregon Swallowtail	Salem
Fort Astoria	County (-ies)	Pacific Golden Chanterelle	Tribe (-s; -al)	Seal

Oregon Bingo: Card No. 26

© Barbara M. Peller

Oregon Bingo

Hudson's Bay Company	Climate	Portland	Executive Branch	Hazelnut
Pear(s)	River(s)	Lewis and Clark	Salem	Basin and Range
Willamette Valley	Tribe (-s; -al)		Oregon Swallowtail	Legislative Branch
Eugene	Border (-ed)	Dr. John McLoughlin	Seal	Agricultural
County (-ies)	Flag	Jory	Thunder-egg(s)	Fort Astoria

Oregon Bingo

Hudson's Bay Company	Executive Branch	Thunder-egg(s)	Portland	Chief Joseph
Hazelnut	Jory	River(s)	Oregon Trail	Flag
Tribe (-s; -al)	Columbia Plateau		Fort Astoria	Motto
Multnomah Falls	Eugene	Metasequoia	Oregon Swallowtail	Salem
Beaver	High Desert	County (-ies)	Seal	Pear(s)

Oregon Bingo: Card No. 28

Oregon Bingo

Jory	Executive Branch	Eugene	Lewis and Clark	High Desert
"Oregon, My Oregon"	Motto	Dr. John McLoughlin	Fort Astoria	Thunder-egg(s)
Industry (-ies)	River(s)		Basin and Range	Portland
Hazelnut	Pear(s)	Judicial Branch	Oregon Swallowtail	Salem
Chief Joseph	Fish (-ing)	Seal	Border (-ed)	Tribe (-s; -al)

Oregon Bingo: Card No. 29

Oregon Bingo

Columbia River	Portland	Oregon Trail	High Desert	Salem
Agricultural	Executive Branch	Hudson's Bay Company	Flag	Basin and Range
Industry (-ies)	Crater Lake		Fort Astoria	Dr. John McLoughlin
Seal	Border (-ed)	Beaver	Oregon Swallowtail	River(s)
Pear(s)	Union	Tribe (-s; -al)	Jory	Thunder-egg(s)

Oregon Bingo: Card No. 30

© Barbara M. Peller

www.ingramcontent.com/pod-product-compliance
Lightning Source LLC
LaVergne TN
LVHW061338060426
835511LV00014B/1998